30 Days of Reflection

Blessing Book

"Twinkle" Marie Manning

Matrika Press

30 Days of Reflection Blessing Book
Copyright © "Twinkle" Marie Manning
April 2020, June 2025

All Rights Reserved
including the right of reproduction,
copying, or storage in any form
or means, including electronic,
In Whole or Part,
without prior written
permission of the author.

ISBN: 978-1-946088-20-8

1.Journal 2.Self Care 3.Self-Exploration
4.Spirituality 5.Philosophy 6.Keepsake 7.Title

Cover Image: Resin art by Joscelyne Drew

Matrika Press

www.MatrikaPress.com
www.RSOTDE.org/MatrikaPress

#LivingLifeAsAPrayer
#PiecesOfPeaceOnEarth

Introduction

Blessing Books are created by "Twinkle" Marie Manning and are a source of intentional inspiration to be used to record personal messages to the owner of the Blessing Book. These mementos and keepsakes can be used in rituals, celebrations and communions as well as for self-reflection and documentation of one's innermost thoughts, feelings and beliefs. At the heart of Blessing Books is the desire to share sentiments, messages and stories that we can draw upon as sources of comfort and a reminder that we are loved. This Blessing Book was created for self-exploration and contemplation.

How to Use the 30 Days of Reflection Blessing Book:

This book is designed to be used as a self-led retreat that you guide yourself on for 30 Days. Each day select a word or phrase that is meaningful to you. Place the word or phrase at the top of selected page. Use the content space provided to describe its significance. The space is kept intentionally small so as to encourage ease of this daily writing. There are daily prompts to serve as guides. Writers can spin off of these prompts or take their daily entry in an entirely different direction.

This Blessing Book is about YOU. It can be used in times of joy or in times of sorrow. It can be used to mark a milestone such as a significant birthday or important season of your life. It can be used to help you process a loss or transition in your life. It can be the place you affirm what is *next* for you as you cross a threshold and visualize your greatest intention for your life. It can be a book of prayers and poems you create.

The *30 Days of Reflection Blessing Book* can also be filled out by you as a gift for another, or as a treasure to be placed in your family's library as a book filled with your own reflections, beliefs, hopes and dreams you wish to pass on to your family.

Wherever you are on your journey, may this Blessing Book serve you well.

For more resources and rituals to accompany this book, including Blessing Stones, visit: **RSOTDE.org/reflection-books**

This Blessing Book belongs to:

_____

Occasion:

_____

Date:

_____

Days of Reflection

Table of Contents

1. _____
2. _____
3. _____
4. _____
5. _____
6. _____
7. _____
8. _____
9. _____
10. _____
11. _____
12. _____
13. _____

14. _____

15. _____

16. _____

17. _____

18. _____

19. _____

20. _____

21. _____

22. _____

23. _____

24. _____

25. _____

26. _____

27. _____

28. _____

29. _____

30. _____

Reflections
Thoughts for Contemplation by the Author
About the Publisher
About the Author
Other Works by this Author
Coming Soon
Resources

"Before I can tell my life what I want to do with it,
I must listen to my life telling me who I am."

— Parker Palmer

What is your life telling you?

Day 1

Date: _____

*"Happiness lies not in finding what is missing,
but in finding what is present."*

— Tara Brach

What gifts are present in your life?

Day 2

Date: _____

"You've got to love what's yours."

— *Alicia Keys*

What is yours?
How do you demonstrate your love for what is yours?

Day 3

Date: _____

"I don't have to chase extraordinary moments
to find happiness - it's right in front of me
if I'm paying attention
and practicing gratitude."

― Brené Brown

What experiences are you most grateful for?

*"One looks back with appreciation
to the brilliant teachers,
but with gratitude
to those who touched our human feelings."*

― Carl Jung

Who are you most grateful for?

Day 5

Date: _____

> "There is a lie that acts like a virus
> within the mind of humanity.
> And that lie is:
> 'There's not enough good to go around.
> There's lack and there's limitation
> and there's just not enough.'
> The truth is that there's more than enough good
> to go around."
>
> ◻ Michael Beckwith

What "good" would you like to manifest in your life?

Day 6

Date: _____

*"My songs are the reflection of how
I think and how I feel
in that moment."*

― Shakira

If your life were a song right now, what would its most relevant lyrics be?

Day 7

Date: _____

*"My belief is that communication
is the best way to create strong relationships."*

— Jada Pinkett Smith

How do you practice effective and compassionate
communication in your relationships?

Day 8

Date: _____

"The mark of spiritual maturity is the ability to deal with paradox."

◻ Rev. Jaelynn Scott

What paradoxes are present in your life?
How have they caused you to grow spiritually?

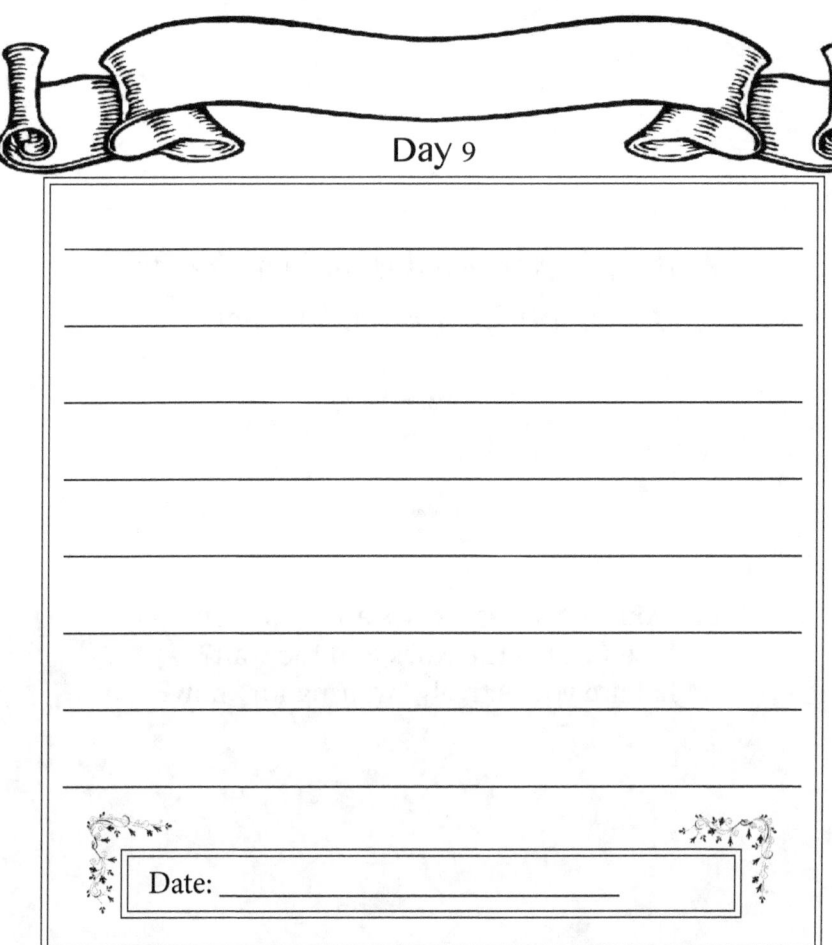

Day 9

Date: _____

*"Waiting is both passive and passionate.
It's a vibrant contemplative work."*

~ Sue Monk Kidd

What in your life's discoveries and experiences have been worth the work and the wait?
What are you actively "waiting for" now?

Day 10

Date: _____

*"When something's ending,
you go through so many phases,
and it can be frustrating.
But once you're out on the other side,
it's like you can really see
all the crazy phases you went through."*

— Norah Jones

What transformations have impacted your life?

Day 11

Date: _____

*"I am balanced at the brink of wisdom.
I'm impatient to receive a new sign."*

— Pat Humphries

What sign are you waiting for?
What intuitive knowing is nudging
at your consciousness?
What direction will your journey take once you grasp it?

Day 12

Date: _____

*"We are born into gratitude:
the knowledge we have received
and the desire to give in turn."*

— Charles Eisenstein

What unique knowledge do you carry with you?

Day 13

Date: _____

*"You wanna fly, you got to give up
the (stuff) that weighs you down."*

— Toni Morrison

What burden do you carry that is heavy?
What is weighing you down that is time to release?
What will shift in your life if you can
let go of this weight?

Day 14

Date: _____

"The truth is, you are strong enough.
The truth is, you are ready now for more.
The truth is, your inner light
is resonant and healing.
The truth is, you are loved,
surrounded by love, filled with love."

— Anna Huckabee Tull

What do you most want to heal within yourself
and within your life?

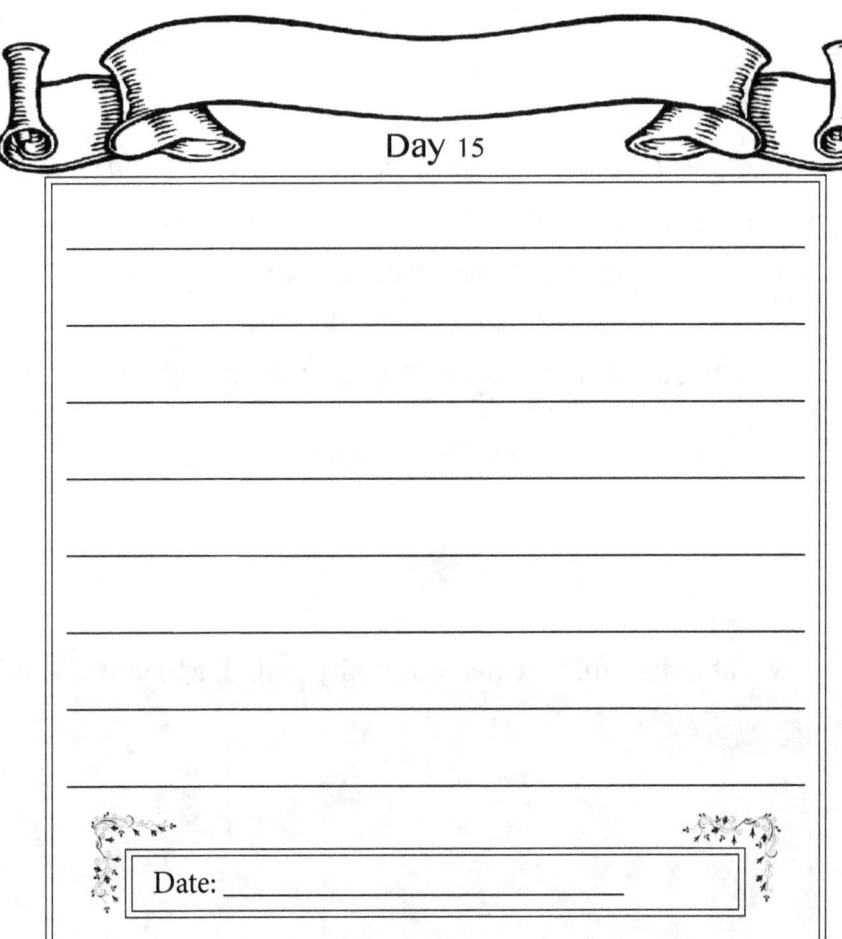

Day 15

Date: _____

"Redemptive work cannot be accomplished alone
because human salvation is not a solo act.
We were not broken alone
and we cannot heal without
the sustaining support of other persons."

— Rev. Dr. Thandeka

What does a fully healed humanity look like to you?

Day 16

Date: _____

> "Many people worry so much about managing their careers, but rarely spend half that much energy managing their LIVES. I want to make my life, not just my job, the best it can be. The rest will work itself out."
>
> — Reese Witherspoon

What is the greatest vision you have for your life?

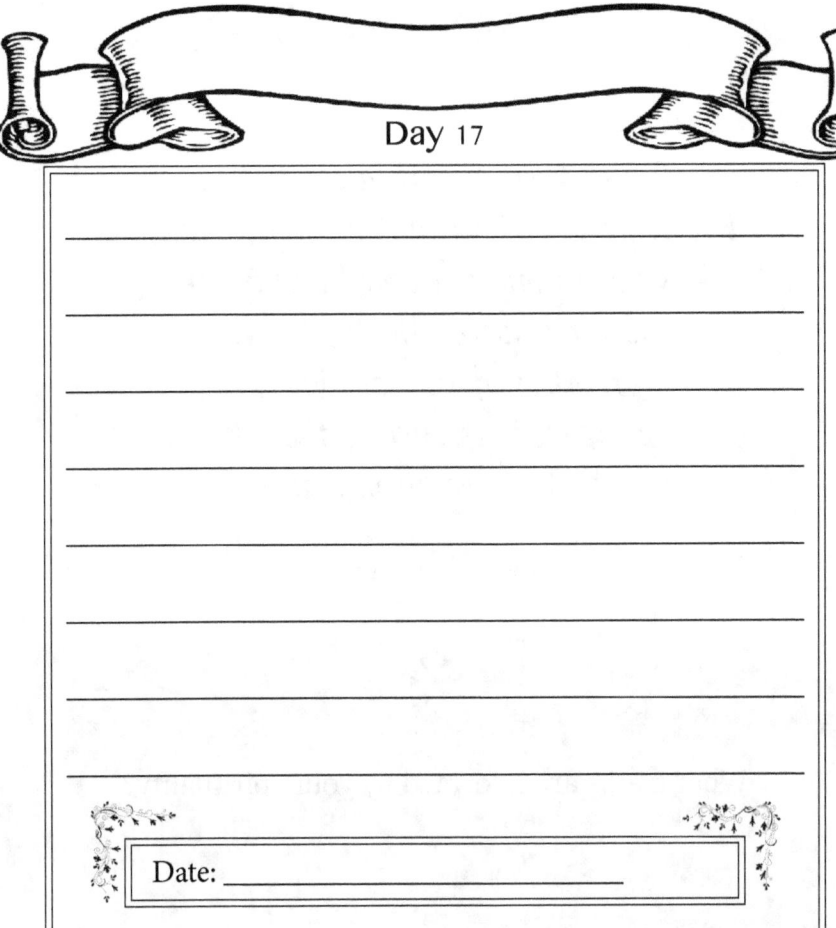

Day 17

Date: _____

> "Truth resides within each of us.
> I've come to believe that authentic truth
> is not so much learned or taught
> as remembered in the deepest
> recesses of the soul (self),
> the ultimate essence of the Spirit
> of which we all partake."
>
> — Rev. Carlton D. Pearson

What truths are informed by your spirituality?

Day 18

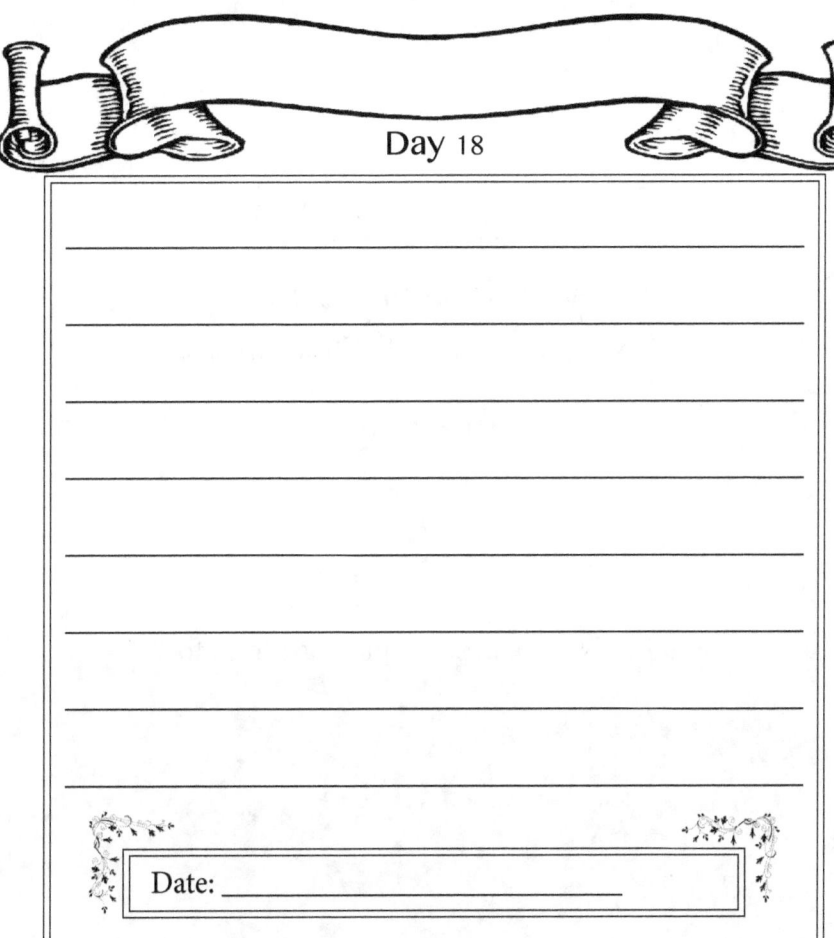

Date: _____

> "I acknowledge my feeling
> and gratitude for life
> by praising the world
> and whoever made all these things."
>
> — Mary Oliver

What in Nature are you most grateful for?

Day 19

Date: _____

"I am one with all the power there is.
I will learn how to contact this power within me!
I will learn how to cooperate with this power!
I will learn how to use this power wisely.
I will keep this power flowing."

    — *Rev. Dr. Della Reese Lett*

What has the power within taught you?

Day 20

Date: _____

"It is our choices that show what we truly are, far more than our abilities."

— J.K. Rowling

Which of your choices uniquely demonstrate the traits that you most wish to be known for?

Day 21

Date: _____

"But then, a grateful heart beats
in a world of miracles.
If I could only speak one prayer for you,
my children, it would be that your hearts
would not only beat but grow ever greater
in gratitude, that your lives, however long they
prove to be and no matter how they end,
continue to bring you miracles in abundance."

— Rev. Kate Braestrup

What are you most grateful for?
What miracles result from such gratitude?

Day 22

Date: _____

"The number one thing you have to do before you set out on any goal or any course is to define your expectations"

— John Mayer

In business, in relationships, in life, you are the only one who can measure *your* success. This is also true of spiritual matters. What does success look like to you?

Day 23

Date: _____

*"People don't buy what you do;
they buy why you do it.
And what you do
simply proves what you believe."*

— Simon Sinek

What's Your Why?

Day 24

Date: _____

*"The well you drink from is
the well you think from."*

— Sandra Dee Robinson

Which well are you drinking from?
How is this evident in your thinking,
speaking, feelings, and actions?

Day 25

Date: _____

> "The way to maintain one's connection to the wild
> is to ask yourself what it is that you want.
> This is the sorting of the seed from the dirt.
> One of the most important discriminations
> we can make in this matter
> is the difference between
> things that beckon to us
> and things that call from our souls."
>
> — Clarissa Pinkola Estes

What is calling from your soul?

Day 26

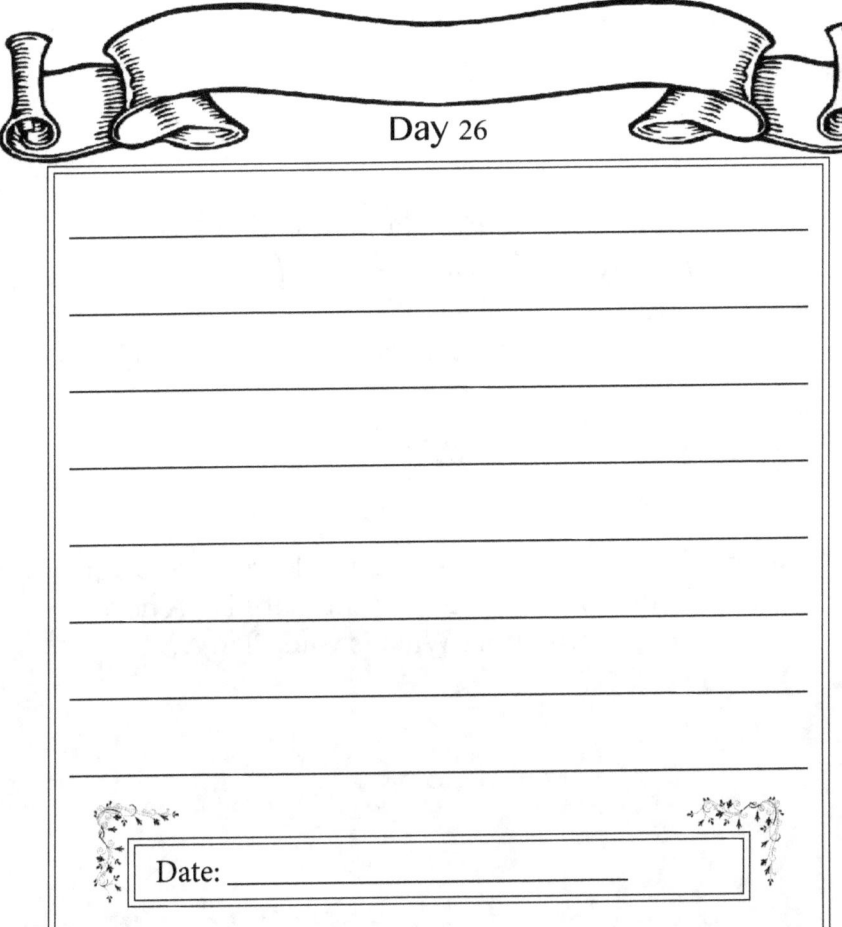

Date: _____

> *"There is no reason to have a Plan B because it distracts from Plan A."*
>
> — Will Smith

Many of us spend our lives doing tasks related to our Plan B's. All too often to the extent that Plan A never gets our attention. What is your Plan A?

Day 27

Date: _____

"Any time an opportunity scares you that much, you should seriously consider saying yes."

– Rob Lowe

What opportunities would you say 'Yes' to if you were unafraid?

Day 28

Date: _____

*"Lighthouses don't go running all over an island
looking for boats to save;
they just stand there shining."*

☐ *Anne Lamott*

What quality about You do you want
to shine the brightest?

Day 29

Date: _____

*"One thing is certain:
We are all on borrowed Time.
Every moment alive, we get to choose
where our Time reserve goes, how we spend it,
and who we allow to draw from it.
Perhaps our greatest responsibility
is truly to be mindful of our Time."*

~ Rev. Dr. "Twinkle" Marie Manning

Where, who and to what do you really want
to dedicate your time?

Day 30

Date: _____

Reflections

What additional discernments have come through to you during these 30 Days of Reflection?

Thoughts for Contemplation
Including musings, poetry, meditations, teachings and prayers.

Listen
Breathe in each morning the magick of Life;
Breathe out each evening deep gratitude for living.
And Listen to the Call of the Universe
in every interaction
in every curve in the road
in every commitment to task
in every covenant of relationship
in every whispered word
in every meditation
in every prayer
in every song
Listen.

May we enter the Holy Quiet:
That place of Being that is within us,
and through us, and beyond us.

Many spiritual practices turn our attention towards the infinite, which can help us see the larger picture of Oneness, yet it can sometimes also serve as a spiritual bypassing of sorts, which can become a habitual distraction, addictive in detaching (or hiding) rather than coping with what is present in our lives.

Bringing it to the finite perspective – which is truly what we have in each given moment – is not only more manageable, but also practical in a spiritual sense because it opens the door to deep gratitude for the life we have, even if we are struggling in the moment, we are present to it and able to do something about it.

May Love be the light
and Grace be the compass
that reveal the way forward.

Consider with me this:

There is a divine echo that whispers
within every heart.
Indeed, that every soul carries with it
the echo of a intrinsic intimacy.
An original echo that is brought fourth
through time from original source.
A primal source where we are all One.
And we carry the essence of this original echo
as a talisman of our divinity.

There exists a place in our hearts where intimacy has
no limit and love has no barrier.

When one listens to the Universe,
the Universe listens back.

Does time echo forward?
Or does it echo back?
It seems to me the latter.
But is it possible to track?
Coincidences coincide continually.
Yet are they purposeful perpetually?
It seems to me quite possibly.
But is this reality?

When the need for silence is great
Yet its soulful sound is filled instead
With errant thoughts granted unguarded audience by
Ego's solicitations to sadness,
Allow your heart to be occupied with
Hildegard's beseeching praise of the Divine;
Allow yourself to immerse in the space
Of such holy tenderness;
Within this musical embrace
You will find silence holds you.

Do you Pray?

I pray daily and throughout the day.
My life is a life of prayer.
My journey with prayer has been
an ever evolving one.
At present prayer to me is surrender and gratitude.
The first, surrender, is in communion with,
and experience of, the Holy.
The second, deep gratitude for the Holy and the
many gifts in my life. The outward appearance of
such prayers can be formal or spontaneous:
intentional moments of stillness and silence, visualization, or active with writing, creating art, chanting
or singing or drawing down the moon, walking in
the woods and along the river, speaking out loud my
heart's desires or giving a blessing, it is the lullabies
with my child each night.…Prayer is even found in
doing the dishes at my kitchen sink,
and dancing in my living room.

May you live Life like a Prayer.

I believe that prayer can be as diverse as that which
we call Holy and can be made manifest through
words, thoughts and deeds, such as daily acts of grace
and gratitude.

I turn to prayer in gratitude and also in surrender
when circumstances are beyond my control. Sometimes my prayers manifest in writings and visualizations; oftentimes the simple act of touching my hand
to my heart and humming (kind of like the Om)
places me in conscious union with the divine.

My guess is, that we each have something that
we feel is Holy. And I urge you to turn to that first.
When feeling vulnerable, when feeling scared,
when feeling like you are just not quite
feeling like yourself,
Turn to that which you identify as Holy,
identify as Sacred.

When we live life as a prayer,
our reactions to situations and to people
become subtle,
even unconscious,
manifestations of the prayer
we bring in to the world.

We begin to recognize the beauty blossoming
in our own hearts and minds.
And as that beauty blossoms,
we recognize with clarity
the callings of our heart;
the *callings* from God.
And it is this,
hearing and answering our callings,
which transforms our otherwise transient lives
into union with the Divine.
This union becomes evident in the transfiguration
of our thoughts,
and our emotions.
And when this happens
we no longer need to clench when faced with
challenging situations
or difficult people.

What if hospitality
was the pillar of our Faith?

If coming together
created sanctuary?

If sharing Joys and Sorrows
was the path to enlightenment?

What if our sacred texts
were our sermons, poems and songs?

If our principles
were our doctrines?

If our covenant
was the Hope that binds us?

Indeed,
What if compassion presided
over our thoughts and our deeds?

Life is center-oriented.

A supportive force, designed
to bring us naturally into alignment.
The catch?
It requires our active participation.
In return, it gives us the needed gravitational pull to center.
It does not require us to reject any part of our selves.
Yet is does demand we have a clear center to orient us.
With that in balance, we can be confident that
we can align all parts as we hold close to our center
with seemingly effortless grace.

The sustainability of the peace, joy, and purpose
we discover in our hearts
is strengthened (and weakened)
by the people and communities we choose
to surround ourselves with.

In myriad ways, we connect and affect.

Whatever is inside of us continually flows outward;
Whatever is outside us continually flows inward.

If life on the outside is presenting
things to be grateful for,
gather the gratitude for those
into your Heart's storehouse.

If life on the outside is presenting things
that cause you to feel fear or sadness,
reach into your heart and find
the place where your love
and your gratitude
and your peace
and peace of mind
resides
and bring that forward.

Because the world needs it.
You need it.

To have resolve is to be gifted
unyielding firmness or endurance.

To practice resolve is to act
with robust commitment that is
made possible by a strong,
healthy, dynamic faith.

May it be known
That I retrieve all I am
To do all I am meant to.
From this moment on.
So mote it be.

May your life be filled with a kaleidoscope of color
and beauty and joy.

May we be like the trees
and transform our world
with every breath.

May deep listening begin to take place from every
corner of each controversial discussion.
Deep listening without accusations.
Deep listening with the goal
of understanding each other.
May we remember we are a people of Love.

May we understand that
we are capable of being loved,
no matter what wounds we still carry,
no matter what mistakes we still make.
May we know that
we are capable of loving generously,
even beyond our wildest imaginations.
May we see
beyond the shadow and into the Soul.
Amen and Blessed Be.

As a society, we treat Time as if we have
a surplus attached to a lavish line of credit
and syphon it into a plethoric gluttony
of distractions.
We are either numb to,
or feel the pressing weight of,
the tedious excess expected of our Time.
Time, a commodity
impossible to trade for its actual value.
Time, a trust fund
we cannot save for a rainy day.
Time, a gift
that comes with freedom of will.
Time, gaining equity
only in legacy.

How important it is to make every moment count.

This Dance of ours, Life's Journey,
consists of
Time and the Choices we make.
Choosing Directions
for our life's course
and
Perpetual Migrations
to live in to those choices.
Some directions are complicated.
Some Migrations are short distances.
We carry from these our memories
and the ramifications
of Time and of Choices.

Every moment alive,
we get to choose
where our Time reserve goes,
how we spend it,
and who we allow to draw from it.

Perhaps our greatest responsibility
is truly to be mindful of our Time.

Instead of one call to action after another,
how about a call to rest,
to be still,
to go within,
to look each other in the eyes,
to hold each other,
to be with one another.

What I am suggesting,
What I'm imploring,
And what I am asking...
...is for you to give yourself permission to rest.

Relax.
Unclench.
Breathe.

Sacred.
Benevolent.
Loving.

Moving forward is necessary;
"moving on" is impossible.

Our loved-one's death was more than a moment;
their life is more than a memory.

Their existence is ever-present
as they shape our lives even now.

The Afterward is a place we all must travel to
on our paths towards wholeness and healing.
The Afterward in not meant to be permanent
Accept that there is more than the Afterward.
There is the Next.
There is Life.
There is Now.

Because we belong together,
we are called to exercise compassion
towards each other,
and, towards ourselves.

It is the act of compassion that awakens us
to bring forth our best gifts to our community.

It is the act of self-compassion that emboldens us
to be brave,
and by 'be brave'
I mean it is self-compassion that allows us
to be vulnerable enough
to give over our burdens and our sorrows
into the tender loving care of our community.

Shared vulnerability,
sharing our most joyful experiences,
along with our sorrows,
this is what builds strength.

Strength in our community.
Strength in each of us.

May we build such Beloved Communities.

Beyond an altruistic "unconditional love"
is the concept of a trusted-love,
an "undoubted love."
The kind of love that is mutually intentional,
mutually experienced.
May we know how to love and be loved in return.

To attain spiritual enlightenment,
spiritual sophistication, spiritual maturity,
requires the full acceptance,
welcoming and claiming of the human experience.
This unequivocally means the integration
of our sexuality into our spirituality.
We are happier, healthier, body, mind and spirit
when we embrace and embody our sacred sexuality.
As such, the energy flowing outward from us
into our relationships and communities
reflects this well-being.

Sabbatical Thinking

If in the fabric of our human lives
we built our organizations,
our communities,
our nations,
with the sentiment that we are indeed One,
we would begin to weave together lifestyles,
and cultures,
and ways of being that support,
and lift up,
nurture and nourish such Oneness.
In such a society,
we would install extended times of rest
and enrichment and sabbatical and retreat.
For everyone.

Love the Land You're With

Doing so creates an embodied relationship with Nature.

If you live near the ocean, you can connect with the resonance of Her rhythms, finding both strength and healing there. Immerse in her wisdom. Enjoy the Oceans' sandy beaches and weathered cliffs. They provide long moments of reflection and inspiration. The metaphysical aspects of our souls open in Her presence. Unimaginable horizons open to us as the inescapable reality of the vastness of Life is before us each day and every night.

Inland you can find lakes and mountains that ground us in this place in Time, while providing us insights on the legacies of those who came before us, and the ones that will follow. In their stillness and aliveness, the mountains, the lake, the land and trees and fields that surround us guide us to embrace a deeper connection with Earth and with Spirit. If you live inward, both literally and symbolically, you can experience an ever-evolving transformation and awakening. Inland Life provides us with the opportunity to grow and to harvest as we work with the soil of the Land. Many find that inland they are nurtured and more nurturing.

Restoring Harmony

When what we recognize as disharmony materializes, especially when the disharmony creates physical isolation from the people we love, the places we like to spend time, and the routines and rituals we've organized our lives around, we can feel deeply disconnected. Disconnected from that which we hold dear. Disconnected from our own self assuredness and self awareness. Disconnected from where we draw our faith. This disconnected feeling feels like chaos to us. Disrupting the harmony we recognize as holy. As sacred. As safe. Yet if we can still the emotional storm that is rising. If we can locate calmness in our bodies, in our beings, we can restore the harmony. As we cultivate this practice of weaving harmony from within the chaos, we become the conductor in the symphony of our emotions. This does not mean the chaos disappears entirely. Nor that we receive answers we like to all the things we have questions about. But it makes space, intentionally so, for us to navigate effectively within what Life has presented us with.

The Peaceable People

Who were the peaceable people?
The tribe whose culture never in all their history oppressed another tribe?
Nor oppressed anyone within their own tribe?
What covenants did they create to facilitate peaceableness?
What race were they?
What color were they?
Which genders were they?
Which lands were sacred to them?
Which deities did they call their own?
Where did they come from?
Where did they go?
Where did they reside when the world was coming apart at the seams?
Where are they now?
Why did their peaceable reign end?
How can we achieve such peaceableness again?
When do we begin?

About the Publisher

Matrika Press is an independent publishing house dedicated to publishing works in alignment with liberal religious Values and Principles. Its fiscal sponsors is Melusine's Haven, a 501c3 organization in collaboration with RSOTDE and Twinkle's Place.

Matrika Press publishes anthologies, memoirs, poetry, prayer and ritual manuscripts, and other books to bring meaning and transformation to the world. A primary goal of Matrika Press is to publish stories and works that would otherwise remain untold. We also resurrect out-of-print manuscripts to ensure our historical works remain accessible.

Why the name "Matrika"?
It is said that Matrika is the intrinsic energy or sound vibration of the 50 letters of the Sanskrit alphabet called "the mothers of creation." The Goddess Kali Ma used the letters to form words, and from the words formed all things. This aligns with scriptures that assert "in the beginning was the Word," and in other sacred texts that affirm people of all backgrounds and faiths agree: Words are powerful. More than that: Their vibrations are creative forces; they bring all things into being.

Matrika Press titles are automatically made available to tens of thousands of retailers, libraries, schools, and other distribution and fulfillment partners, including Amazon, Barnes & Noble, Chapters/Indigo (Canada), and other well-known book retailers and wholesalers across North America, and in the United Kingdom, Europe, Australia and New Zealand and other Global partners.

For more information, visit:

www.RSOTDE.org/reflection-books

About the Author

    Rev. Dr. "Twinkle" Marie Manning is an interfaith minister, skilled ritualist and liturgist who has been leading workshops and seminars in the secular and spiritual worlds for more than two decades. She actively develops and leads programs that nourish spirituality. Her rituals, reflections and poetry have been included internationally in all manner of worship services and publications.

    The series of Reflection & *Blessing Books* is the newest of her publishing endeavors. Other published works include the *Women of Spirit* anthology series, *Intentional Visualization, Be Like the Trees, Restore Us to Memory,* and the *Pulpit of Peace* collection. Upcoming works include *Anam Ċara and The Divine Echo,* and *Living Life as a Prayer manual and workbooks.*

    Her community ministry, affectionately known as *Twinkle's Place,* is her home-base where she hosts a variety of retreats and spiritual programs.

www.RSOTDE.org/titles-by-twinkle-marie-manning
www.EmpoweringWomenTV.org/founder
www.TwinklesPlace.org

Other Works by this Author

www.RSOTDE.org/women-of-spirit-series

Women of Spirit, Exploring Sacred Paths of Wisdom Keepers is a compilation of women sojourners, sages, mystics, witches, shaman, medicine women, ministers, philosophers, therapists, life coaches, yogis, and more.
Their journeys.
Their stories.
Their teachings and practices.
Essays, Poetry, Art, Rituals and Prayers.
This anthology is full of useful tools and powerful messages for everyone who is on a spiritual journey to embrace and enjoy. Beloved Contributors include:

- *Anna Huckabee Tull*
- *Bernadette Rombough*
- *Deb Elbaum* • *Deborah Diamond*
- *Debra Wilson Guttas* • *Grace Ventura*
- *Janeen Barnett* • *JoAnne Bassett*
- *Judy Ann Foster* • *Julie Matheson*
- *Kate Early* • *Kate Kavanagh*
- *Katherine Glass* • *Kris Oster*
- *Lea M. Hill* • *Meghan Gilroy*
- *Morwen Two Feathers* • *Rustie MacDonald*
- *Shamanaca* • *Sharon Hinckley*
- *Shawna Allard* • *Shiloh Sophia*
- *Susan Feathers* • *Tiffany Cano*
- *Tory Londergan*
- *"Twinkle" Marie Manning*
- *Tziporah Kingsbury* • *Valerie Sorrentino*

Women of Spirit, Transforming Lives is the second volume in the Women of Spirit Series.

Beloved Contributors include:
- Anne B. Gass
- Anya Searle
- Arica Walters
- Beth Amine
- Carole Fontaine
- Cheryl Partridge
- Danielle Dufour
- Deana Sanderson
- Erin Colene
- Fatima Al-Sayed
- Jaishree Dow-Spielman
- Jane Sloven
- Kiana Love
- Leana Kriel
- Melissa Kennedy
- Mika Leone
- Pam Swing
- Patricia Diorio
- Sloane Reali
- Tam Veilleux

Curated by:
"Twinkle" Marie Manning

Coming Soon...
Women of Spirit Volume Three!!

www.RSOTDE.org/women-of-spirit-series

Pulpit of Peace: *Inspirational Quotes from a Prophetic Ministry*

This book features excerpts from Rev. Dr. "Twinkle" Marie Manning's sermons, as well as glimpses of her poetry, meditations, rituals and reflections. Common themes of her ministry and writings found in this book include: Building The Beloved Community; Möbius Life; Explorations of Divinity; Living Life as a Prayer.

Pulpit of Peace is part of the *a Pocketful Book Series*.

Be Like the Trees *(a Sermon in My Pocket)* speaks candidly about tragedy, grief, and challenges faced in daily life. Rev. Dr. "Twinkle" Marie Manning's words weave together a beautiful collage of insights and inspirations as she directs us towards the interconnectedness and magic of our human existence.

Coming Soon to the "a Sermon in My Pocket" series:

Restore Us to Memory
explores remembering (and reclaiming) who we are and offers encouragement to live our lives in such a way that we will be remembered how, and as who, we want to be remembered as.

Anam Ċara and The Divine Echo
centers a mystical aspect of belonging, and practical ways to demonstrate such belonging in our lives.

www.MatrikaPress.com

Goddess Guardian
Oracle Cards

Designed by: "Twinkle" Marie Manning

Published by
MATRIKA PRESS

www.TwinklesPlace.org/GoddessCards

Surf & Earth Designs

Joscelyne Drew is an award winning artist and one of the pioneers in ocean and abstract themed resin art. Her years of experience developing a distinctive beautiful technique and formulas have achieved a look that is like no other. Her work has been included in shows spanning from the Florida keys to Maine.

Joscelyne's abstract and contemporary nautical, reef and earth elements inspired resin art is also ideal for tables and bar-tops.

Commissions and custom orders of any size are welcomed!

www.facebook.com/SurfandEarthDesigns

Participate in one of Empowering Women TV's *Signature Events*

and/or Join Our Team and Host
Empowering Women events in your community!

www.EmpoweringWomenTV.org
www.EmpoweringWomenTV.org/join-our-team

Join "Twinkle" Marie Manning on Patreon and Substack!

www.Patreon.com/LivingLifeAsAPrayer

www.Substack.com/@PiecesOfPeaceOnEarth

Kindly make a donation to support Twinkle's work:

@TwinkleMarie

RSOTDE

www.ingramcontent.com/pod-product-compliance
Lightning Source LLC
Chambersburg PA
CBHW081726100526
44591CB00016B/2514